Mastering Affiliate Marketing

Strategies for Digital Growth and Business

Earl.J.Mark

Table of contents:

Introduction

chapter 1
   Understanding the basics of affiliate
marketing

Chapter 2
   Exploring partner Programs and systems

Chapter 3
   Creating compelling substances for
transformation

Chapter 4
   Optimizing SEO for affiliate Success

chapter 5
   Maximizing affiliate Growth with
strategics social media intégration

chapter 6
   Achieving Success

Introduction

Affiliate marketing - Power Path in the Vast Landscape of Digital Business. In today's interconnected world, the opportunities to monetize your passion, expertise or platform have expanded exponentially. Affiliate marketing emerges in this sea of opportunity, providing a gateway for people to harness their creativity, entrepreneurship and digital prowess in their pursuit of financial freedom. Affiliate marketing is essentially a collaborative enterprise where symbiotic relationships between creators, marketers and consumers come together to form a mutually beneficial ecosystem. Imagine forging alliances with established brands or innovative products, acting as a channel to seamlessly connect those offerings to receptive audiences looking for solutions or value. But affiliate marketing isn't just about promoting products—it's an art form that requires strategic thinking, nuanced communication, and a keen understanding of audience needs. It's about creating engaging content that captures, informs and ultimately compels action. It understands the psychology behind consumer behaviour and uses various digital channels to drive traffic and results - from social media storytelling to search engine visibility optimization. However, success in affiliate marketing is not just about joining programs and sharing links. It requires commitment, persistence and an insatiable desire to learn and adapt. The digital marketing landscape is constantly strengthening and requires constant vigilance to stay ahead of trends, algorithms, and consumer preferences. On this journey, we'll explore the intricacies of affiliate marketing, discover strategies for success, consider the nuances of effective advertising tactics, and delve into the mindset needed to succeed in this dynamic arena. Together we embark on a transformative journey of discovery, unlocking secrets, strategies and limitless possibilities in the exciting world of affiliate marketing.

Chapter 1

Understanding the Basics of Affiliate Marketing

Discovering the Pillars of a Profitable Partnership at the core of affiliate marketing is the fundamental relationship between consumers and adopters. This synergy creates a profitable environment where affiliates act as intermediaries, facilitating the promotion of products or services offered by merchants to potential consumers.

Main components:

- **Partners**: affiliates, also known as publishers or partners, are the driving force behind the affiliate marketing ecosystem. These individuals or communities create content, run platforms or build audiences through blogs, websites, social media or other digital media. Their primary function is to promote products or services through unique referral links provided by merchants.

- **Marketers (promoters or sellers):** Marketers are companies or individuals offering products or services that want wider visibility and more sales. They work with affiliates and provide them with special tracking links or promotional materials. Merchants benefit by contacting affiliates and established audiences, leveraging their reach to increase brand visibility and sales.

- **Consumers:** Consumers, the ultimate target group, are individuals who are looking for solutions, products, or services. They consume content created by affiliates click on the affiliate links in the recommendation or recommendation and then make a purchase. These activities generate income for both the affiliate and the merchant.

Key Dynamics and Actions.Affiliate Links and Tracking: Affiliates receive unique tracking links from merchants. These links contain identifiers that track consumer actions related to the affiliate (such as clicks, conversions or sales). Advanced tracking mechanisms ensure that they correctly calculate the commission for the affiliate and its advertising performance.

- **Commission Structures:** Affiliates earn commissions based on merchant-predetermined structures. These structures vary from fixed commissions per sale to percentage-based commissions. Some programs offer tiered systems that encourage affiliates to achieve higher sales volumes with higher commissions.

- **Content Creation and Promotion:** The cornerstone of successful affiliate marketing is creating interesting, valuable and authentic content. Affiliates use a variety of strategies—reviews, tutorials, comparison articles, videos, or social media posts—to resonate with their audience and drive results.

Key Notes and Consideration when creating contents

- Compliance and Disclosure: Compliance with legal and ethical guidelines, such as disclosure of affiliate relationships, is critical. Transparency builds trust and credibility by ensuring ethical marketing practices.

- Choosing profitable niches and programs: Strategically choosing niches and programs that match the affiliate's expertise, audience interests and market demand is key. Research and analysis help identify profitable opportunities.

- Constant Learning and Adaptation: The affiliate marketing landscape is constantly growing. Staying abreast of industry trends, consumer behaviour and technological advances is critical to continued success.

Understanding the basic principles of affiliate marketing lays the foundation for a successful business. Armed with this knowledge, aspiring affiliates can begin their journey with the strategies, ethics and knowledge needed to build rewarding partnerships, engage audiences and grow revenue through affiliate marketing. Understanding these basics lays the foundation for a successful affiliate marketing journey, creating a sound foundation for navigating the dynamic landscape of partnerships and profit productivity..

Chapter 2

Exploring Partner Programs and Systems

A Comprehensive Direct to Profitable Associations. The complicated web of associate promoting calls yearning business people with guarantees of inactive salary and entrepreneurial independence. However, inside this sweeping domain lies a significant viewpoint that frequently decides an associate marketer's success—the craftsmanship of exploring partner programs and systems.

Divulging the associate biological system:Associate programs serve as the foundation of this energetic industry, acting as bridges interfacing with associates and shippers. These programs, encouraged by dealers or associate supervisors, offer an organized stage where partners get the items, get special materials, and gain commissions through performance-based promotion.

Understanding Partner Programs:Associate programs come in different forms—ranging from personal dealer programs to member systems lodging different dealers and offers. The individualized programs regularly coordinate organizations with particular brands or businesses, advertising interesting items or administrations. Alternately, member systems total numerous dealers beneath one umbrella, giving partners a wide cluster of offers inside a single stage.

Exploring Member Systems: Associate systems work as centralized centre points, rearranging the method for partners to investigate and connect different programs inside a single interface. These systems streamline operations by giving plenty of dealers, assorted specialities, solidified announcing, and frequently standardized installment forms, lessening regulatory overhead for associates.

Components Impacting Program Determination:

- **Item Pertinence and Arrangement:** Choosing programs adjusting to an affiliate's speciality, and gathering people's inclinations, and skills is significant. This guarantees substance consistency, improving engagement and transformation rates.

- **Commission Structures and Payout Models:** Assessing commission rates, installment recurrence, and payout edges helps in selecting programs advertising profitable gaining possibilities and convenient installments.

- **Dealer Validity and Back:** Collaborating with legitimate vendors advertising quality products/services and vigorous member back cultivates belief and encourages smoother collaborations.

- **.Navigational Methodologies for Victory:** Careful Investigate and Due Tirelessness: Conducting in-depth investigation, perusing program surveys, and comprehensively understanding program terms and conditions mitigates dangers and upgrades decision-making.

- **Expansion and Experimentation:** Testing different programs or systems, broadening associations, and analyzing execution measurements empower partners to distinguish high-performing roads and optimize procedures.

- **Relationship Building and Communication:** Setting up compatibility with partner supervisors, looking for direction, and cultivating proactive communication develops stronger partnerships and opens entryways to elite openings.

- **Grasping Advancement and Adjustment:**The associate showcasing scene is liquid, stamped by ever-evolving shopper behaviours, showcase patterns, and innovative headways. Remaining dexterous and versatile is paramount—regularly assessing, optimizing methodologies, and grasping inventive approaches guarantees maintained significance and victory.

Acing the craftsmanship of exploring partner programs and systems enables partners to manufacture strong organizations, maximize income streams, and explore the complexities of this flourishing industry. It's an undertaking of disclosure, methodology, and innovation—travel where educated choices, tirelessness, and versatility lay the foundation for maintainable victory within the energetic domain of partner promoting. Exploring member programs and systems is associated with charting a course in a tremendous ocean of openings. This guide offers a compass to assist partner marketers in exploring these waters, controlling them towards beneficial organizations and maintainable development.

Chapter 3

Creating Compelling Substance for Transformations:

The ability to create enticing content is a key factor in achieving success in the fast-paced world of affiliate marketing. Crafting content that not only locks in but convinces gatherings of people to require activity is an art—craftsmanship that, when aced, can drive significant changes and income for associate marketers.

The interesting Substance:

- **Locks in Narrating:** Narrating rises above unimportant advancement; it captivates and reverberates with groups of onlookers on an enthusiastic level. It's approximately weaving accounts that interface, teach, and entertain—instigating interest, whereas consistently joining member offerings into the narrating circular segment.

- **Value-Centric Approach:** Conveying esteem is the

foundation of interesting substance. Whether it's through instructive articles, solution-driven guides, or engaging recordings, a substance must offer substantial benefits, tending to the gathering of people's torment focuses and giving arrangements.

- **Genuineness and Dependability:** Genuineness breeds belief. Veritable, straightforward substance builds validity, cultivating a sense of belief between the partner and their group of onlookers. Unveiling member connections and giving fair conclusions are essential in developing enduring beliefs.

Methodologies for Substance Creation:
- **Understanding Gathering of People Needs:** Exhaustive gathering of people inquiring about discloses experiences into inclinations, interface, and torment focuses, permitting partners to tailor content that reverberates

profoundly with their group of
lookers.

- **SEO Optimization:** Coordination
  of significant catchphrases, meta
  portrayals, and optimizing
  substance for look motors
  upgrades perceivable, drawing in
  natural activity and expanding the
  gathering of people's reach.

- **Visual and Mixed media
  Request:** Joining outwardly
  engaging components such as
  pictures, infographics, or video
  substance hoists engagement,
  making complex data edible and
  vital.

- **Conversion-Oriented
  Substance Strategies:** Call-to-
  Actions (CTAs): Clear and
  compelling CTAs provoke activity.
  Making influential CTAs
  deliberately put inside substance
  guides groups of onlookers
  towards wanted actions—be it

clicking member joins, marking up, or making a buy.

- **Benefit-Focused Dialect**: Highlighting the benefits and esteem suggestions of member items or administrations instead of fair highlights, lures groups of onlookers and drives changes.

- **Social Confirmation and Tributes:** Joining veritable tributes or social proof—reviews, supports, or user-generated content—adds validity and fortifies the product's adequacy.

- **Moral Contemplations and Compliance:** Adherence to moral rules is vital. Unveiling associate connections, maintaining a strategic distance from tricky hones, and keeping up straightforwardness brace the belief between members and their group of onlookers. Maintaining moral benchmarks not complies with directions but to jam long-term connections.

- **Grasping Cycle and Optimization:**Substance creation is an iterative process. Analyzing measurements, examining a group of onlookers' behavior, and A/B testing different content designs, styles, and procedures empower members to refine their approach, ceaselessly upgrading substance viability.

Crafting an interesting substance that changes over is an amalgamation of inventiveness, sympathy, and vital consideration. It's travel where understanding a group of onlookers' subtleties, conveying esteem, and cultivating belief crosses to form an immersive encounter. When associates ace this creation, they open the potential for sustained engagement, transformations, and victory within the competitive scene of affiliate marketing. Creating substance that changes over isn't almost influence; it's about delivering esteem and building belief. This directly engages member marketers to use the control of interesting substances, changing

casual perusers into locked-in buyers and faithful
advocates.

Chapter 4

Optimizing SEO for Affiliate Success

Increase Visibility and Boost Conversions Search Engine Optimization (SEO) in a vast and highly competitive digital environment for your audience's attention.Mastering is a success.

At its core, SEO is a strategic approach that goes beyond ranking high in search engine results in increasing visibility, attracting organic traffic, and boosting affiliate marketing conversions.

SEO Foundation:

- **Keyword Research and Analysis:** Keyword research serves as the foundation of SEO. Understanding search intent, identifying relevant long-tail keywords, and studying user queries in your niche are the foundation for creating content that resonates with your audience and complies with search algorithms.

You can improve the readability and user experience of your website by optimizing content elements like meta title, description, header, and

URL structure. It's important to align your content to the search query while ensuring readability and relevance.

- **Quality Content Creation:** Content quality is a top priority in SEO. Interesting, informative, and valuable content not only attracts your audience but also attracts other websites to link to, increasing authority and trustworthiness, which are important factors in search engine rankings.

- **Strategic Affiliate SEO Tactics:** Niche-Specific Targeting: Tailoring your content to a specific niche builds authority and relevance, drives targeted traffic interested in your affiliate offers and also helps attract audience

- .**Building Backlinks:** Maintaining high-quality backlinks from trusted sources improves your rankings and visibility by validating the authenticity of your content and demonstrating authority to search engines.

Optimizing your content for mobile devices helps it reach more people using smartphones and tablets, making it easier for them to access and improving their experience while also boosting your search rankings.

Leveraging SEO Tools and Analytics:

- **SEO Tools:** By leveraging a variety of SEO tools, including keyword research tools, analytics platforms, and SEO plugins, affiliates can gain insights, track performance, and improve their strategies.

- **Interpret your analytics:** Analyzing metrics like organic traffic, click-through rates, bounce rates, and keyword performance provides actionable insights to help you adjust your strategy and content optimization.

- **Adapting to SEO trends and algorithm updates:** SEO is a dynamic situation. It's important to stay on top of algorithm updates, developing search trends, and new SEO practices. Adaptability ensures sustainable relevance and competitiveness in search engine rankings.

- **Ethical SEO Practices:** Adhering to ethical SEO practices promotes sustainable growth. Avoiding black hat tactics, prioritizing user experience, and following search engine guidelines are essential to long-term success.

- **Bottom line:** Optimizing SEO for affiliate success not only improves search rankings but also creates a holistic digital experience. It's a synergy of technical dexterity, content expertise, and audience-oriented strategy.

When an affiliate uses his SEO as a foundation, the potential to increase visibility, attract qualified traffic, and increase conversions is unlocked, ushering in an era of sustained success in the affiliate marketing environment.

SEO optimization is not a one-time effort. It's a continuous journey of refinement and adaptation.

This comprehensive guide provides affiliate marketers with the tools and strategies they need to harness the power of SEO and pave the way for increased visibility, engagement, and conversion-driven success.

Chapter 5

Maximizing Affiliate Growth with Strategic Social Media Integration

In the rapidly growing digital marketing environment, harnessing the power of social media has become an essential strategy for driving affiliate growth.

Integrating your affiliate marketing efforts with social media platforms provides an entry point to a wider audience, increasing engagement and increasing conversions.

Successfully leveraging social media for affiliate growth requires a nuanced approach that includes several key elements.

From creating engaging content for different platforms to cultivating genuine relationships with your followers, every aspect contributes to building a powerful presence in the affiliate space.

- **Create engaging content:** It's essential to create customized content that resonates with your audience on social media platforms. By creating high-quality, value-driven content, you can align your users with their preferences and behaviours to ensure maximum impact and engagement.

- **Building Authentic Connections:**Transparency, authenticity, and trustworthiness are at the core of building a loyal following. Building genuine relationships with your followers builds trust and increases the likelihood of influencing their purchasing decisions.

- **Strategic Partnerships:** Working with influencers and content creators increases your visibility and credibility within your target market. Expand your affiliate marketing efforts by working with people who share your brand's values and have a passionate following.

- **Data-driven optimization:** Analytics and performance tracking tools allow you to measure the effectiveness of your campaigns. Analyzing metrics, such as engagement rates, conversion rates, and ROI, helps you make informed decisions and optimize your future strategy.

- **Adaptability to trends:** It's important to stay on top of developing social media trends and algorithm changes. Adapting your strategy based on platform updates ensures relevance and sustained success in a dynamic digital environment.

Chapter 6

Achieving Success

Email Marketing Strategies to Increase Sales In the digital marketing realm, email marketing is a mainstay among countless strategies to attract audiences and increase sales.

Email marketing is a great tool for driving sales and nurturing customer relationships because of its ability to directly reach your audience, deliver customized content, and foster personalized connections. It will continue to be.

- **Segmentation and Personalization:** The foundation of effective email marketing is segmentation and personalization.

Dividing your subscriber base into segments based on demographics, preferences, and purchase history allows for targeted messaging.

Customizing content that resonates with each segment creates a sense of personal connection, increasing engagement and increasing conversions.

- **Engaging Content and Engaging Copy:** Creating engaging content and engaging

copy is key to attracting attention
in a crowded inbox.
A concise but effective subject line, combined with
engaging and relevant content in the email body,
will encourage recipients to open the email, read it,
and take the desired action.
Providing value through informative, entertaining, or
educational content will encourage recipients to
interact with your email and your brand.

- **Mobile Optimization:** I opened
  Most emails on mobile devices, so
  optimizing your emails for mobile
  responsiveness is non-negotiable.
  Ensuring your emails look good on a variety
  of screen sizes and devices ensures a
  seamless user experience, leading to
  increased engagement and higher
  conversion rates.

- **Automated Workflows and Drip
  Campaigns:** Leverage automation
  with drip campaigns and
  automated workflows to optimize
  your customer journey.
  By sending timely, targeted emails based on
  user behaviour or predefined triggers,
  businesses can nurture leads, re-engage

dormant customers, and move prospects down the sales funnel.
which can ultimately lead to conversion.

- **Social Proof and Urgency Tactics:** Including social proof elements such as testimonials, reviews, and user-generated content increases the credibility and trustworthiness of your promotional emails.

Additionally, using emergency strategies like limited-time offers, countdowns, and exclusive sales can help drive sales by creating a sense of urgency that prompts recipients to take immediate action.

- **A/B Testing and Data Analysis:** Continuous improvement is at the core of a successful email marketing strategy.

A/B testing distinct elements, such as subject lines, CTAs, images, and content, to find what resonates best with your audience.

Analyzing key performance metrics, such as open rates, click-through rates, conversion rates, and unsubscribe rates, provides valuable insights that can help you improve and optimize future campaigns.

Effective email marketing strategies that increase sales are diverse and dynamic.
 By leveraging segmentation, personalization, engaging content, mobile optimization, automation, social proof, A/B testing, and data analytics, businesses can unlock the true potential of email marketing and engage subscribers.
 We can foster meaningful connections and deliver tangible results in the following ways: achieve more sales and profits.

Chapter 7

Growing Your Success

Leveraging Paid Advertising for Profitable Campaigns In the digital age where competition for consumer attention is fierce, paid advertising helps businesses expand their reach, increase conversions, and ultimately has become an important tool for improving profitability.
 When used strategically, paid advertising can generate impressive returns on investment and pave the way for profitable campaigns that help your company achieve its goals.

*Strategic Targeting and Segmentation:*The core of any successful paid advertising campaign is strategic targeting and segmentation.
 Accurately identifying and targeting the right audience based on demographics, interests, behaviour, or previous interactions ensures that your advertising efforts resonate with users most likely to convert.
 Segmentation enables customized messaging that speaks directly to specific audience segments, maximizing relevancy and engagement.

Engaging Ad Creative and Messaging:Creating engaging and creative and engaging messaging is essential to standing out in a crowded digital environment.

Eye-catching images, concise and effective copy, and a clear call to action (CTA) can be a persuasive way to get viewers interested in your ad and take the desired action, such as making a purchase or signing up for a service.

Optimize for different platforms and formats:With the variety of platforms and add formats available, it's important to optimize your campaigns for each specific platform.

Whether it's search ads, social media ads, display ads, or video ads, tailoring your ad content to the nuances of each platform increases visibility, improves the user experience, and increases the likelihood of conversion.

Data-driven decision-making: Leveraging data analysis and insights is critical to refining and optimizing paid advertising campaigns.

Analyzing key performance indicators (KPIs) such as click-through rate, conversion rate, cost per acquisition, and return on a spend can provide valuable insight into the effectiveness of your campaigns.

This data-driven approach allows you to make informed decisions and allocate resources to the most effective strategies.

Testing and Iteration: Continuous testing and iteration is an important part of a successful paid advertising campaign.

A/B testing different ad elements, such as headlines, visual elements, targeting parameters, and CTAs, can help you find what resonates best with your target group.

Iterating on these insights refines your campaigns, improves performance, and maximizes return on investment.

Budget Allocation and Monitoring: Efficient allocation and monitoring of advertising budgets is of paramount importance.

Continuously evaluating and adjusting budgets based on key performance indicators ensures optimal use of resources.

Additionally, careful monitoring allows you to timely identify underperforming ads and channels and make quick adjustments to reduce losses and capitalize on opportunities.

A multifaceted approach is required.
When implemented carefully and iteratively, paid advertising can be a powerful source of revenue, helping businesses achieve their goals and grow in today's competitive digital environment.

Chapter 8

Analytics and Tracking

Maximizing Performance in the Digital Space In the dynamic space of digital marketing, the ability to derive actionable insights from data analysis and tracking mechanisms has become essential.
 Analytics and tracking serve as a compass to guide organizations toward informed decision-making, allowing them to optimize strategy, improve user experience, and ultimately drive performance to unprecedented heights.

Comprehensive Data Collection: The foundation of effective analysis and tracking lies in comprehensive data collection across a variety of touchpoints.
 Capturing a wide range of data points, from website interactions and social media interactions to email interactions and progress through the sales funnel, gives you a complete picture of user behaviour and preferences.

Key Performance Indicators (KPIs) and Goals:Determining relevant key performance indicators and setting clear goals are critical to measuring success.

Whether it's conversion rate, click-through rate, customer acquisition cost, or engagement metrics, aligning KPIs to higher-level business goals allows you to measure performance and effectively track progress.

_Advanced Analytics Tools and Technologies: Advanced analytics tools and technologies enable businesses to gain actionable insights from massive data sets.
Platforms like Google Analytics, CRM systems, heatmaps, and social media analytics tools enable deep analysis, pattern recognition, and predictions to facilitate informed decision-making.

Segmentation and Personalization: Segmentation of data enables targeted marketing initiatives and personalized user experiences.
Segmenting your audience by demographics, behaviours, and interests enables customized messaging and content delivery, driving deeper connections and higher engagement rates.

Attribution Modeling: Understanding the customer journey through attribution modelling is important for assigning value to different touchpoints.

Whether you use first-touch, last-touch, or multi-touch attribution models, attributing conversions to specific interactions allows you to allocate resources more effectively and optimize your marketing efforts.

Continuous testing and optimization: A culture of continuous testing and optimization based on data insights is essential for sustained success. A/B testing different variables such as B. Creatives, landing page layouts, or email subject lines allow iterative improvements to fine-tune your campaigns for maximum impact will be done.

Real-time monitoring and adaptability:Real-time monitoring of analytical data allows you to quickly adapt to changing trends and unexpected changes. When organizations are agile and responsive to new insights, they can capitalize on opportunities or immediately mitigate problems, promoting agility and resilience in a rapidly changing digital environment.

Data Protection and Compliance:maintaining data protection and complying with regulations (such as GDPR and CCPA) is of paramount importance.

Ethical data collection, storage, and use practices not only build trust among consumers but also reduce risks associated with data breaches and non-compliance.
Analytics and tracking form the foundation of a successful digital strategy, enabling businesses to make informed decisions, improve performance, and deliver a superior user experience.

By harnessing the power of comprehensive data collection, advanced analytical tools, segmentation, continuous optimization, and ethical practices, businesses can navigate the complexities of their digital environments, maximize performance, and ultimately achieve their goals.
achieve your goals and gain an edge in today's competitive market.

Chapter 9

Maximizing Commissions and Partnerships Strategically

In affiliate marketing and business partnerships, negotiating higher commissions and fostering profitable partnerships is a skill that can have a significant impact on profits and growth.
 A strategic and sensitive approach to negotiation can pave the way for mutually beneficial agreements, move companies toward their goals, and foster long-term, profitable relationships.

- **Understand value propositions:** Successful negotiations depend on a thorough understanding of the value proposition each side offers.

Before entering into discussions, understanding the unique strengths, audience reach, and benefits that both parties bring will provide the basis for developing interesting proposals that highlight the shared value of partnership.

- **Data-Driven Performance Analysis***:* Demonstrating past performance and data-driven results is essential to demonstrating the potential of a partnership. Providing evidence of successful conversions, high engagement rates, or increased sales from previous collaborations will inspire confidence and strengthen the case for negotiating commission rates or higher incentives.

- **Identify win-win scenarios***:* Effective negotiations revolve around identifying win-win scenarios where both sides have every opportunity to gain significant value.

Developing propositions that highlight clear benefits for both parties, whether through increased visibility, reaching new audiences or revenue growth, lays the foundation for a collaborative partnership that cooperates with common goals.

- **Leverage unique selling propositions:**Highlighting your unique selling propositions (USPs) and differentiators is essential in negotiations. Emphasizing what sets a company apart, whether it's niche expertise, cutting-edge technology, exclusive access or exceptional customer service, strengthens your negotiating position and justification for higher commission requirements or more favourable conditions.

- **Building relationships and trust:**Investing time in building relationships and nurturing trust is the foundation for successful negotiations. Establishing transparent communication and a genuine interest in your partner's success will foster a collaborative environment conducive to reaching mutually beneficial agreements.

- **Explore performance-based models:**Explore performance-based models, such as revenue sharing or tiered commission structures tied to specific milestones, possibly bringing common benefits. Pairing incentives with performance measures not only minimizes risk but also ensures that they directly link rewards to measurable results.

- **Negotiation techniques and flexibility:**Use negotiation techniques such as active listening, compromise, and finding creative solutions that allow for flexible negotiations. A willingness to explore alternative arrangements or change terms based on the partner's needs can often lead to a more favourable outcome for both parties.
- **Legal clarity and documentation:**Formalize agreements through clear, legally binding contracts that protect the interests of both parties.

Ensuring that contractual agreements include all negotiated terms, fees, performance metrics and termination provisions will provide a solid foundation and minimize potential future disputes.

Chapter 10

Strategies for Scaling and Diversifying Your Affiliate Business

In the ever-changing affiliate marketing landscape, the ability to scale and diversify operations is essential for sustainable growth, increased revenue streams, and resilience to market fluctuations. Adopting strategic approaches to expansion and diversification allows affiliate marketers to open up new opportunities, expand their reach, and strengthen their business to achieve long-term success.

Expansion through niche diversification:Diversification into multiple niches or sub-segments allows for expansion of the target market.

- Explore related niches that help attract a broad audience
- Leveraging existing expertise, content strategy, and marketing tactics to penetrate new markets.

Scaling content creation and SEO strategy:Scaling content creation is integral to reaching a broader audience and improving organic visibility.

Applying effective content production processes, investing in an SEO strategy, and creating quality, green content across various platforms will improve visibility, attract organic traffic money and establish power over many niches.

Exploring new traffic sources and platforms:Venturing into new traffic sources and platforms will expand the reach of affiliate businesses.

While maintaining a powerful presence on established platforms, exploring emerging social media platforms, paid advertising channels, influenced collaborations, podcasts or marketing videos opens the doors to new audience segments and diverse traffic streams.

Scaling products and services: Scaling up by diversifying the range of products or services promoted allows for a broader monetization strategy.

Expanding your product line, promoting higher-priced items, or exploring different affiliate programs will diversify your revenue streams, reducing dependence on a single product or program.

Establish partnerships and strategic alliances: Collaborating with industry partners, influencers, or complementary businesses will enhance reach and credibility.

Forming strategic alliances through partnerships not only expands the audience base but also facilitates cross-promotion, knowledge sharing and access to markets or customer segments of new products.

Invest in automation and technology: Scaling effectively includes leveraging automation and technology to streamline operations.

Deploy affiliate management software, automate email campaigns, use analytics tools to make data-driven decisions, and apply a CRM system that improves productivity and scalability. Broaden and optimize marketing efforts.

International expansion and localization: Going global by tapping international markets and localizing content will expand a company's reach.

Tailoring content, language, and marketing strategies to suit different cultural nuances and preferences will ensure relevance and resonance across different regions.

Continuous testing and optimization: Adopting a culture of continuous testing and optimization is critical to successful scaling.
A/B testing different strategies, analyzing performance metrics, and iterating on data insights help refine and improve marketing initiatives across different channels and niches.

Risk mitigation and adaptability: While scaling and diversification are necessary, risk mitigation and adapting to market changes are essential. Monitor performance metrics maintain flexibility to respond to changes in consumer behavior or industry trends and have contingency plans in place to help mitigate risks associated with expansion.

Scaling and diversifying your affiliate business requires a multifaceted approach that includes diversifying your niche, expanding your content, discovering new traffic sources, product expansion, strategic partnerships, automation, internationalization, continuous optimization, risk mitigation and adaptability.
By implementing these approaches strategically, affiliate marketers can navigate the complexities of expansion, open alternative growth paths, and position their businesses for success.

Conclusion:

Master affiliate marketing for endless digital possibilities. In the digital startup space, success depends on mastering affiliate marketing.

As we wrap up this transformative journey with "Mastering Affiliate Marketing: 4,444 Digital and Business Growth Strategies," it's clear that this is more than just a book; it's the gateway to endless possibilities in the digital landscape.

Armed with Earl J.

Mark's expert advice, you now have a treasure trove of strategies, tactics, and principles that will enable you to direct your affiliate marketing efforts toward unprecedented success.

This book is more than just learning;

By demystifying the complexities and revealing the intricacies of affiliate marketing, Earl has ensured that you have a roadmap to navigate this dynamic terrain with confidence and expertise.

Whether you're new or a seasoned marketer, the principles shared here are widely influential and lay the foundation for sustainable business growth in the digital age.

So, as you close the last pages of "Mastering Affiliate Marketing", remember that this is not the end but the beginning of your journey towards full realization. The potential of affiliate marketing.

Take these lessons, apply them diligently, and watch your digital aspirations transform into remarkable achievements.

Congratulations on embarking on this rewarding journey to mastering affiliate marketing, where every step taken brings you closer to unlocking the countless opportunities that await you in the tech industry and digital business .